Eugenie Clark, Shark Lady

by Kendra Adams

D1711695

Chapter 1
A Scientist

Eugenie Clark is a famous scientist. She has spent her life studying fish. Sharks are some of her favorite fish. Eugenie has traveled around the world to learn about different kinds of sharks. Many people call Eugenie Clark the "shark lady."

Eugenie Clark carries an explorer's flag underwater for a film about the small fish shown here.

Three Kinds of Sharks

lemon shark

hammerhead shark

great white shark

Chapter 2
Observing Fish

When Eugenie was a young girl, she spent hours observing fish at the New York Aquarium. Eugenie learned about different kinds of fish, and she pretended she was in the water with them. She wondered what it would feel like to be one of the fish.

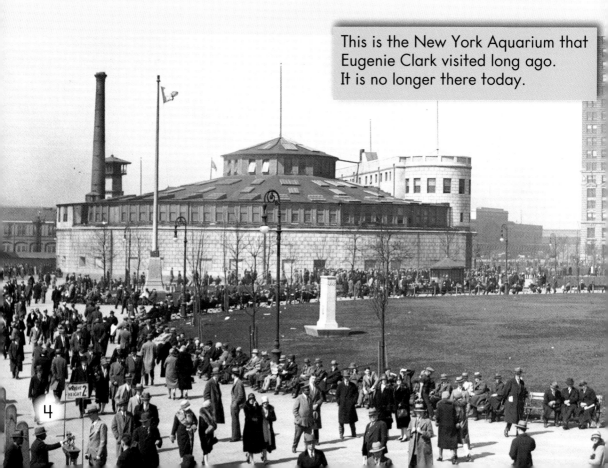

This is the New York Aquarium that Eugenie Clark visited long ago. It is no longer there today.

At home, Eugenie set up her own fish tank. She watched her fish carefully and took notes about what they did. She wrote about fish and read about them. It was her dream to become a scientist someday.

This model of a shark sits outside the popular New York Aquarium of today.

Chapter 3
A Fish Expert

Not many women were scientists when Eugenie was young. But that didn't stop her. When Eugenie went to college, she took science classes and became a fish expert.

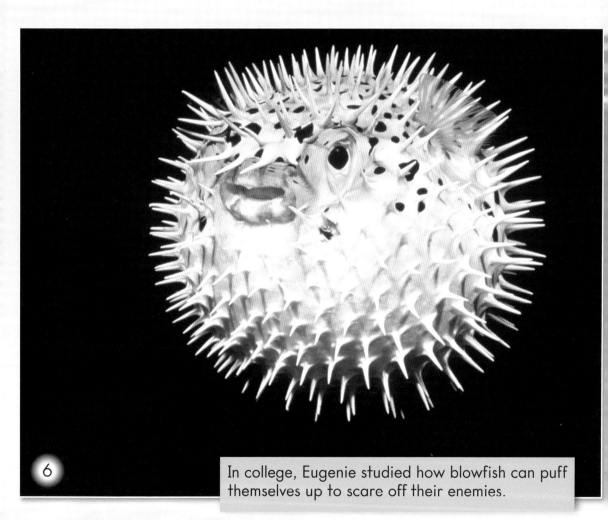

In college, Eugenie studied how blowfish can puff themselves up to scare off their enemies.

Eugenie Clark studies a shark up close.

Eugenie decided to dive deep in the sea, so she could study fish where they live. She learned how to dive with a mask and how to use underwater breathing equipment.

The first time Eugenie saw a shark under the water, she was surprised. The huge shark swam right past her. Eugenie thought it was beautiful, and she was sorry when it swam away.

Chapter 4
Setting Up a Lab

Eugenie traveled to different parts of the world to study fish. She wrote about her work and became a well-known scientist. Then she was asked to start a lab in Florida. The lab was a place where Eugenie and other scientists could study fish.

Scientists study sea life at the Mote Marine Laboratory. Visitors can go to the aquarium there.

A diver watches a lemon shark swimming inside a cage.

In the lab, Eugenie tested lemon sharks to see how smart they were. Eugenie trained the sharks to do things. The sharks learned to ring a bell to get food.

Before this, people thought sharks were not very smart. Eugenie proved that sharks are smart after all!

A diver studies a great white shark from the safety of a cage.

Eugenie Clark says that she is not afraid of sharks. She is too interested in them to be scared. But she also says it is important to understand how sharks act.

Great White Sharks

- Great white sharks can swim fast.

- These sharks have about 5,000 sharp teeth.

- Great white sharks don't chew their food. They tear it off in chunks and gulp it down.

- Seals and sea lions are some of the sharks' favorite foods.

Eugenie used an underwater cage to study great white sharks. These sharks can be dangerous to people, but Eugenie studied them from inside the cage where she was safe. She observed the sharks and took pictures of them.

Chapter 5
Riding a Whale Shark

Eugenie even went for a ride on a whale shark, the biggest fish in the sea. She grabbed the shark as it swam by her. Then she tried to sit on the shark's back, but she couldn't stay on.

A diver swims up close to a whale shark.

Eugenie slid down and held on to the shark's tail for as long as she could. The shark swam faster and faster. But Eugenie did not feel scared.

Finally, Eugenie had to let go. As she watched the huge shark swim away, she felt happy. Eugenie had learned what it felt like to be a shark!

Chapter 6
Sharing Her Work

Eugenie Clark has spent her life studying sharks and other fish. She loves to share what she has learned about them. She talks to scientists and students who visit her lab. She writes books, and she writes articles for magazines, too. Eugenie hopes that other people will love learning about the sea.

Eugenie Clark teaches some children about a shark.

Some Things Eugenie Clark Has Learned About Sharks

- Sharks are smart animals.
  They remember what they learn.

- Sharks eat many kinds of sea animals.
  They eat fish, crabs, and even other sharks.

- Most sharks are timid and stay away
  from people.